A Civilization Project Book

NORTH AMERICAN INDIANS

BY SUSAN PURDY
AND CASS R. SANDAK

Illustrations by Hal Frenck
Diagrams by George Guzzi

A GROLIER COMPANY

Franklin Watts   New York/London/Toronto/Sydney   1982

Contents

Library of Congress Cataloging in Publication Data

Purdy, Susan Gold
  North American Indians.

  (A Civilization project book)
  Includes index.
  Summary: Briefly discusses Indian tribes and cultures of North America. Provides instructions for craft projects, including sand painting and clothing.
  1. Indians of North America—Juvenile literature. 2. Indian craft—Juvenile literature. [1. Indians of North America. 2. Indian craft. 3. Handicraft] I. Sandak, Cass R. II Title. III. Series.
E77.4.P87   1982   745.5′08997   82-8323
ISBN 0-531-04451-3   AACR2

A Rich and Varied Heritage

The Indians are the native peoples who lived in North, Central, and South America before the Europeans came. They were the original occupants of the land where modern cities, factories, farms, and houses now stand.

The Indians included an enormous variety of tribes. In North America alone, there were more than 250 tribes who spoke over a thousand different dialects and many distinct languages. North, Central, and South America cover vast areas of land with a wide variety of climates and terrains. The Indian tribes who inhabited these different areas all developed distinctive ways of life, adapted to their surroundings and the available materials.

However, this remarkable diversity of New World peoples all shared some basic physical features. Dark eyes, straight black hair, and skin colors ranging from coppery red to yellowish tan are all attributable to a common origin. The ancestors of the Indians crossed from northern Asia into the Western Hemisphere via the Bering Strait at different times beginning more than thirty thousand years ago. Separate waves of migration apparently account for the many different linguistic families. Scientists think that by about 8000 B.C. the Indians had spread throughout the Americas.

The people who crossed from Asia brought a New Stone Age type of culture with them. Most Indian groups made fire with a bow and drill, crafted tools out of stone, wove baskets, and dom-

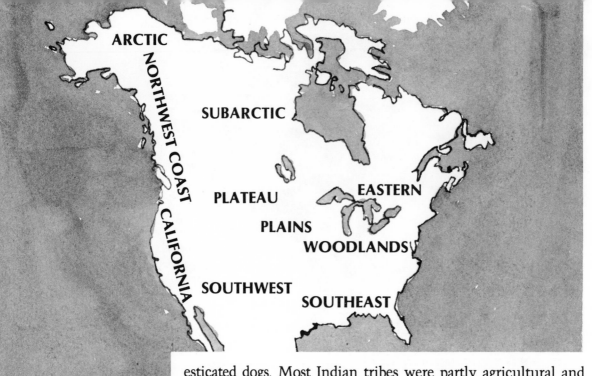

ARCTIC

NORTHWEST COAST

SUBARCTIC

CALIFORNIA

PLATEAU

PLAINS

EASTERN

WOODLANDS

SOUTHWEST

SOUTHEAST

The major North American Indian nations

esticated dogs. Most Indian tribes were partly agricultural and partly dependent on gathering, hunting, and fishing. Indian agriculture was generally based on corn, or maize. Several cultures of Central and South America, including the Mayan, Toltec, Aztec, and Incan, reached high levels of material progress and left impressive architectural and artistic remains.

The Indians of North America can be divided into nine major cultural areas: Eastern Woodlands, Plains, Southeast, Southwest, California, Plateau, Northwest Coast, Arctic, and Subarctic. Within each of these divisions there was a similarity in way of life and livelihood, but there were variations in dress, language, laws, customs, and beliefs.

Sometimes life for the tribes in a certain geographic area revolved around a single species of animal that provided food, clothing, shelter, and other needs. The Plains Indians developed a culture based upon the buffalo. They lived in tepees made from buffalo hide, ate buffalo meat, and wore clothing made from buffalo skin. For the Indians of northern Canada, the caribou was the most important animal.

Some Plains tribes lived in settled villages and farmed the land. Other tribes were nomadic and set up tepees wherever they camped. These Indians, including the Cheyenne, Arapaho, Blackfoot, Crow, and Comanche, battled most fiercely against white settlers. The tribes of the Pacific Northwest lived by hunting, trapping, and fishing for salmon.

Indians lived in many different types of homes. The Eastern Woodlands Indians made houses out of bark. The Pueblos of the Southwest created multistoried apartment houses out of mud bricks. The Pawnees, Omaha, and other Plains tribes built sturdy, round, earth lodges. The Osages had oval, domed houses covered with skins and mats. Some Indians made grass houses. The Navajos of Arizona, New Mexico, and Utah lived in cone-shaped houses called *hogans,* which were covered with bark and mud.

All Indian tribes developed their own special arts and crafts forms. Everyday objects as well as ritual items were made with care and skill and showed the Indians' sense of design and workmanship.

The Indians did not share a common religion. Various Indian tribes worshipped the sun, the rain, the wind, plants, animals, and spirits of ancestors. They tried to please these various beings by means of private prayers and public ceremonies.

The Indians taught the white man a great deal about survival in the wilderness of the New World. Many everyday items come from the Indians, including corn, maple syrup, tomatoes, potatoes, moccasins, snowshoes, and toboggans. Some of these objects are still called by their Indian names. And Indians gave the names to many states, cities, towns, rivers, lakes, and other geographical features throughout the Americas.

It is estimated that in 1492 there were a million Indians in all of North America north of Mexico. Today there are still about a million Indians living in the United States and Canada. But few Indians today are able to live exactly as their forefathers did— relying on hunting, fishing, and light agriculture to supply their needs.

Most modern Indians on reservations in North America support themselves through farming, forestry, and stock raising. Many Indians work in mines or factories or in construction. Some tribes receive money for use of their lands and mineral rights. A large number of Indians practice the traditional crafts: making rugs, blankets, jewelry, pottery, baskets, and beadwork. Increasing numbers are building careers in business, in the professions, in sports, and in the arts. North American Indians are both an exciting part of our history and a vital part of American culture today.

Navajo Sand Painting

Many tribes of the Southwest make sand paintings, especially the Navajos. Sand painting is sometimes called "dry painting." The traditional technique uses powdered minerals and charcoal, as well as dry vegetable materials like pollen or corn meal.

The Pueblos use dry earth pigments to paint stylized pictures on the floors of their holy places during certain rites. The Navajos have expanded on this idea, using colored sand as well as pigments to make symbolic pictures to accompany their chants and ceremonies. Sometimes the sand paintings are used for curing illnesses and other times for bringing rain to assure good crops. Different motifs are used for each purpose. Between 600 and 1,000 separate designs have been categorized.

Sand painting ceremonies often last more than a day, and sometimes up to nine days. A different sand painting is made each day. Before sundown, at the end of each day's

STAR

FROG

rites, the painting of the day is destroyed. A new one is made the next day.

Special rituals are connected with the actual sand painting. The artists (the medicine man or his helpers) use only their right hands to apply the pigment. Sometimes a dozen or more people work most of a day to complete the painting. The painting begins with the design of the central motif and then progresses toward the outer edges. Designs range from 1 to 20 feet (0.3 to 6.1 m) in diameter. The colors used in sand painting symbolize directions: white means east, yellow is west, black is north, and blue is south. Red represents the sun. Women are drawn with square heads, men with round heads. Often, symbols for earth man and woman are shown, with the four holy plants: corn, squash, beans, and tobacco.

A rainbow or striped band in the form of a rainbow girl surrounds three sides. This symbolizes the protection of the sky. The eastern side of the painting is usually left open, that is, not guarded by the rainbow. Here one sees other protective symbols such as the medicine man's "bundles" of sacred healing instruments used to guard the "opening" of the painting.

When sand paintings are part of a healing ceremony to cure an illness, the patient sits on the finished sand painting. Parts of the painting are placed on his or her body. The sick person gains power from the deities or symbols shown in the painting, and the sickness is absorbed by the sand. The sand is ceremonially buried at the end of the day when the design is destroyed.

SQUASH

CORNSTALK

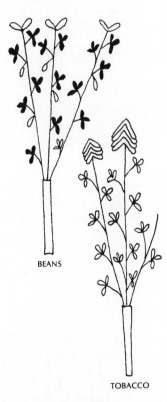

BEANS

TOBACCO

Sacred Navajo Plants Used in Sand Painting Motifs

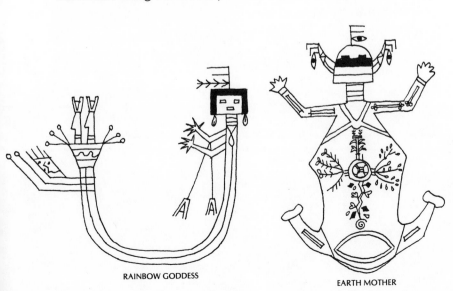

RAINBOW GODDESS

EARTH MOTHER

7

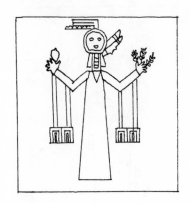

Figure 1

Materials you will need:
A large, flat piece of sandpaper, at least 12 inches (30 cm) square for base, scrap paper, pencil, tape, paper cups or bowls, spray varnish, colored sand (from hobby or pet stores), beach or mason's sand, powdered spices and herbs such as paprika, salt, pepper, cinnamon, turmeric, or dry mustard

1. Plan your design on scrap paper. Follow the traditional motifs or make up your own, as shown in Figure 1.

2. Outline your design on the sandpaper with pencil.

3. Put each color in a separate paper cup or bowl. To pour the sand easily, make several small cones or funnels out of paper and tape them closed. Put a different color in each cone, and tap gently to release the colored pigment, as shown in Figure 2.

4. Use your fingers or the paper cones to "drip" the color over the lines, as shown in Figure 3.

5. To preserve a design, spray it several times with spray varnish.

Figure 2

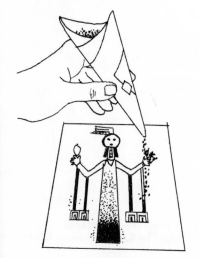

Figure 3

Indian Dancers' Forehead Rosettes

A rosette is an ornament used on Indian headgear. There are a great variety of rosette styles, but basically each rosette consists of a center plaque decorated with paint, beadwork, a mirror, or a disk with brass studs on it. This central plaque is surrounded by one or two rings of colored feathers or horsehair.

Indian dancers of many tribes wore headbands decorated with distinctive rosettes. Some headbands were decorated with a single rosette placed in the middle of the forehead. Others had two rosettes, one over each temple.

Feather rosettes had diameters of 4, 6, 8, or 10 inches (10, 15, 20, or 25 cm). Dancers most commonly used the 4-inch (10-cm) size. A feathered headband with a rosette helps make a colorful, traditional Indian costume.

Woodlands Indians preferred rosettes made of horsehair, usually dyed red, with mirrored center plaques. Dancers often wore these on bracelets as well as on beaded head-bands.

Materials you will need:
Twenty feathers of one color, twenty to twenty-five feathers of a contrasting color, two feathers about 6 to 8 inches (15 to 20 cm) long, felt or cardboard, string,

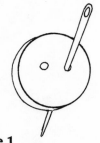

Figure 1

Figure 2

Figure 3

Figure 4

button thread or embroidery floss, darning needle, scissors, glue, brass paper fasteners, pencil, ruler, paints, ribbon headband

1. Cut three circles, each 1½ inches (3.75 cm) in diameter, out of the felt or cardboard.

2. Cut two circles, each 2 inches (5 cm) in diameter.

3. Hold the large pair and the small pair together, and use a needle or tip of a pair of scissors to punch two holes ½ inch (1.25 cm) apart (Figure 1) in the center of each pair. Do not poke holes in the single remaining small circle. This is the base for the central rosette plaque.

4. Place one circle from each pair flat on the table.

5. Glue feathers in a circle on one large and one small piece with the stems pointing in, the tips pointing out (Figure 2). Glue the pair of large feathers on the larger ring. Do not get glue in the center holes.

6. Spread more glue over the feather stems. If you prefer, you can sew the feathers onto the circles the way the Indians did.

7. Cover the stems of each feather ring with the correct size circle. Line up the holes on the top and bottom pieces (Figure 3).

8. Press on the top circle. You now have one large and one small circle of feathers.

9. Allow the glue to dry.

10. Trim the feather tips of each ring, using scissors to cut the feathers in an even fringe. The fringe should extend 1 inch (2.5 cm) beyond the felt or cardboard circle (Figure 4). Do not cut the two long feathers. Just push them inside while you trim the shorter feathers on the larger ring.

11. To make the central rosette plaque, sketch a design, following the suggested pattern (Figure 5) onto the single small circle.

12. Paint your design.

13. Use the brass fastener in the center of the design. Push it onto the middle of the circle from the outside, so the legs will open on the side that can't be seen. Flatten the legs of the paper fastener, and cut off the tips if they stick beyond the edge of the rosette.

Figure 5

14. Place the larger feather ring flat on the table. Center the smaller ring on top of it.

15. Thread a needle with a double thickness of thread or embroidery floss. Stitch through the holes as shown in Figure 6 so that the thread goes over the top of the small circle and the thread legs begin and end on the back side of the largest circle.

16. Tie the threads together in a knot on the back of the largest circle. Leave two 8-inch (20-cm) long threads hanging down, so you can fasten the rosette to the head-band.

17. Place the feather rings so that the small one faces up.

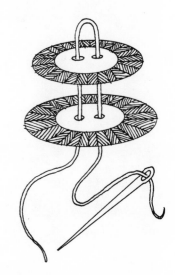

18. Glue the rosette plaque to the center of the smaller feathered ring with the two tall feathers pointing straight up (Figure 7).

Figure 6

19. Tie and/or glue the rosette onto a plain or decorated ribbon headband and wear it.

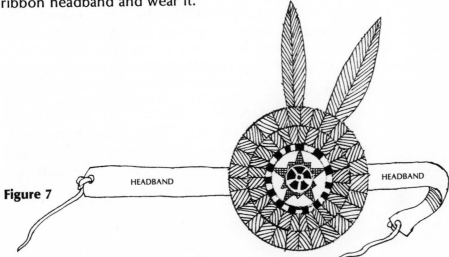

Figure 7

HEADBAND

HEADBAND

Pacific Northwest Coast Totem Poles

The Northwest Pacific Coast Indians placed great importance upon rank. In order of rank, there were chiefs of the tribe, chiefs of the clan, and chiefs of houses. Several households together formed a clan. Sometimes clans were made up of groups who shared a totem animal whom they believed to be an ancestor. Ravens and eagles were symbols, or totems, of the Haida. The eagle, wolf, raven, and bear were totems of the Tsimshian. The wolf and raven were totems of the Tlingit.

Totemism meant that men were closely related to certain animals or mythological beings. Men wanted to possess the same qualities the animals had. Only some animals were used for totems. The Indians who hunted and fished for certain animals made totems of other creatures.

Totem poles followed the basic form of the tree trunk. Both abstract and realistic designs were used. Large individual figures were often shown standing, while other, smaller figures were often seated, their poses stylized and compressed into a symmetrical front or side view. Identifying characteristics represent each creature. For example, the beaver always has large front teeth; the hawk has a large curved beak; the eagle, a beak turned downward. Killer whales have large heads and mouths; the bear shows paws and sometimes holds a stick. Stylized features, such as eyes, paws, or feet, are often repeated. Rounded rather than angular forms were generally used. The wood carvings were often painted.

Totem poles were not worshiped, they were honored, much as we honor the flag. Carved and decorated poles were also used as house posts and mortuary poles. Mortuary poles sometimes contained the body of a dead chief, but usually they supported a wooden box containing his ashes.

House posts supported the roof and interior walls. They were decorated with carvings of family crests. Some poles also served as house signs, to tell who lived inside.

Materials you will need:
Self-hardening clay, or a cylinder 3 inches (7.5 cm) in diameter and 12 inches (30 cm) high of balsa or other soft whittling wood, penknife or modeling tools, tempera paint and brushes, pencil, sandpaper

1. Prepare clay or wood, making a cylinder at least 3 inches (7.5 cm) in diameter and 12 inches (30 cm) tall.

2. With a pencil, divide the cylinder into segments (see Figure 1). In each section, draw a figure. Make sketches on a piece of scrap paper to plan your design. Use figures at random, or try to tell a story with them.

3. Sketch the basic outline of the forms within each segment (Figure 2).

4. Use your knife or modeling tools to carve the forms. Keep the shapes of your figures bold. Use paint to add details. Give the most attention to the characteristics of the head. The legs and arms are usually shown, stylized, in a crouch position. (See Figure 3 for ideas.)

5. When you have finished your carving, sand the rough areas if needed.

6. Paint the totem pole to finish your design.

Figure 1

Figure 2

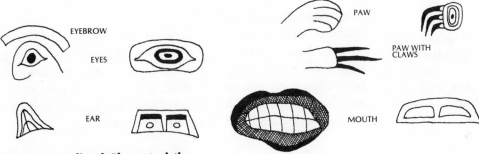

EYEBROW

EYES

EAR

PAW

PAW WITH CLAWS

MOUTH

Figure 3 Stylized Characteristics

13

Indian Pictographs

Indian languages are more figurative and poetic than English. The spoken language is the basis for the pictographs and hand sign language that most tribes also used. Pictographic symbols follow the same sequence of thought as the spoken or gestured language. Smoke signals were sometimes used to transmit messages. Most of the signs used were devised privately, but the signs meaning help, danger, trouble, etc., were used universally.

Picture writing, like sign writing, is a way of expressing thoughts without words. Much thought went into each symbol to make it properly expressive. Petroglyphs (rock carvings) show the most ancient Indian picture communication. Petrographs are writings on rocks; pictographs are picture writings done on skins, bark, pottery, wood, etc.

Study the pictographs given. Then try to invent your own pictographs. Use them to tell your own story. Our project is a pictograph story drawn on a piece of hide.

To read the pictograph, begin at the bottom and read clockwise: Many bows and arrows hit Indian camp. See Bear Gladheart make tracks. Antelope fears man.

Materials you will need:

Piece of tanned hide or leather or suede (use smooth side) or heavy paper such as oaktag or brown wrapping paper cut in the shape of a hide, paints and brushes or permanent ink felt pens, chalk, pencil and paper, nails and hammer or stapler, two forked sticks, a cross-brace stick long enough for hanging the hide

1. Write a very simple story, leaving space beneath each line of words for you to draw the pictographs that correspond to each word or group of words.

2. On another piece of paper, lightly sketch a wide spiral, using chalk. Leave enough space to draw your pictographs between the lines.

3. Paint or write your pictograph story along the lines of the spiral, beginning at the center (Figure 1). Write clockwise, following the circular path to the end.

4. Erase the chalk lines.

5. Try reading the story. Begin at the spiral center and read it clockwise until you get to the end.

6. On an actual hide, lightly sketch a spiral with chalk. (See Figure 2.) Use a color similar to the color of the hide so it doesn't show.

7. Along the spiral, copy your pictograph story with paints or pen.

8. Test a spot to see that your pictographs are completely dry. Erase the chalk lines.

9. Nail or staple the hide to the cross stick (Figure 3). Use the hide as a wall hanging by adding hanging strings (Figure 4).

10. You may want to place the forked sticks in the ground and hang the cross stick across the forks (Figure 5) for display.

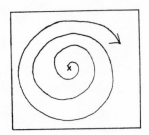

Figure 1

Figure 2

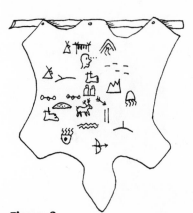

Figure 3

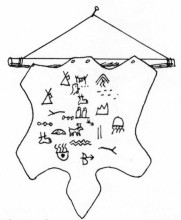

Figure 4

Figure 5

Dance Rattles and Bell Strips

Indian music was primarily vocal. Their chief instruments were of the percussion type—drums and rattles. Some tribes used wind instruments—various types of flutes and whistles. Indian songs were often a form of prayer for rain, health, or victory in battle.

Dance Rattles

Most Indian dancers shook rattles to the rhythm of their dances along with drumbeats or instead of them. Rattles were made from a wide variety of materials. The Cherokees and Pueblos used dried gourds. The Plains Indians used rattles made from steer horn on a string threaded through a stick. The Cherokees often used box turtle shells which, when dried, made fine rattles. The Hopi made a drum-type rattle with a handle, and the Woodland Indians of the Northeast made cylindrical rattles covered with birch bark.

Our model is a simple cylindrical rattle made from a tin can with a wooden handle. The exterior design can be selected from among the motifs of many Indian tribes.

16

Materials you will need:

One feather, thread, 6 oz. (170 gr) or 12 oz. (340 gr) juice can, punch-type can opener, nail, hammer, small pebbles or dried beans, masking or adhesive tape, paper, scissors, glue, crayons or paints, brushes, strips of real birch bark (optional) that you find on the ground. Do not strip any bark from a living tree!

For the handle: a wooden stick roughly ¾ inch (1.9 cm) in diameter and 6 or 7 inches (15 or 17.5 cm) long

1. Use a punch-type can opener to make a hole in the can to remove the juice.

2. Wash out the can and dry it well.

3. Tape the hole closed.

4. In the center of the opposite end of the can, hammer several nail holes (Figure 1), puncturing the can in a small circle just large enough to poke the stick in. Whittle one end of the stick handle into a sharp point.

5. Turn the can over and use a nail to puncture a small center hole for the narrow tip of the stick. Test to make sure the stick fits snugly (Figure 2). Then remove the stick.

6. On colored paper or birch bark, draw circles around the ends of the can, as in Figure 3.

7. Cut out the two circles.

8. Measure the height of the can, and cut a strip of paper or bark this width and long enough to wrap around the can with a slight overlap.

9. Cut out the strip.

10. Draw or paint designs on the strip and on the end circles. For ideas, see Figure 4.

11. Glue the circular bark or paper end panels onto the can. Glue the strip around the can sides, overlapping the ends slightly.

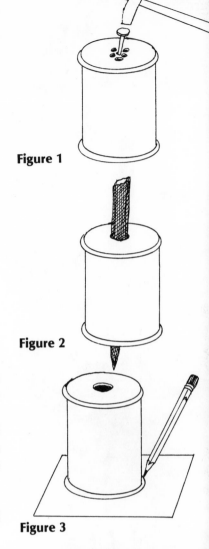

Figure 1

Figure 2

Figure 3

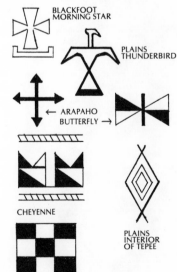

BLACKFOOT
MORNING STAR

PLAINS
THUNDERBIRD

← ARAPAHO
BUTTERFLY →

CHEYENNE

PLAINS
INTERIOR
OF TEPEE

Figure 4   Indian Motifs

Figure 5

12. Take a nail and poke it through the end panels into the holes made for the stick handle. Do this neatly so that you do not rip the paper.

13. Put several pebbles or beans into the can through the hole you made for the handle.

14. Poke the stick handle through the can.

15. If the handle is too loose, wrap the handle with tape to thicken it at the points where it goes through the can. The tip of the stick should extend about ½ inch (1.25 cm) beyond the top of the can.

16. Tie the thread around the feather. Then attach it to the tip of the stick (Figure 5). Use glue to hold the thread in place.

Dancing Bell Strips

Many Indian dancers wear strips of bells to accent their movements, along with, or instead of, rattles. Indian dancers prefer brass sleigh bells, which have a clear, loud ring. They are heavy and require sheepskin padding on the reverse side of the bell strip. For our models, we will use suede or felt with smaller tin bells found in hardware or novelty stores. Bell strips can be worn around the ankles, wrists, waist, or calves.

Materials you will need:
Tape measure, suede or felt, ribbons or strong yarn, scissors, embroidery needle and button thread, bells (Use the heaviest quality tin bells you can find. The number you use will depend on the length of the strip you are making. Try to use at least eight to a strip.)

1. Measure the distance around your waist, ankles, calves, or wrists (or wherever you want to wear the strips). Write down the measurements.

2. Cut strips of suede or felt as long as you need and about 2 inches (5 cm) wide.

3. Make one hole about 1½ inches (3.75 cm) in from each end of each strip, and tie on a ribbon or yarn fastening string (Figure 1).

4. Sew evenly spaced bells along the length of the strips (Figure 2).

5. Tie the bell strips over your clothes, using ribbon or yarn strings.

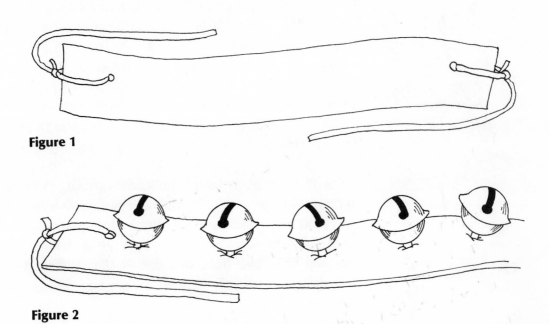

Figure 1

Figure 2

Plains Indians' Parfleche

The Plains Indians carried things in parfleches and pouches of various sizes. A parfleche is a rawhide carrying case; the word comes from the French and means rawhide. A parfleche is made from a rectangular piece of hide that is decorated on the outside. It is then folded up to form a large envelope that is tied together to secure it.

Parfleches are much larger than pouches. The average size for a parfleche is about 1 to 3 feet (30 to 90 cm) long and 6 to 18 inches (15 to 45 cm) wide. Miniature ones were used for pocket carrying. Pouches range from 6 to 18 inches (15 to 45 cm) long and are folded like envelopes (see Figure 7).

The Plains Indians used pouches for carrying items and for ceremonial purposes. Pouches and parfleches were decorated with traditional patterns, often called "parfleche decoration." These patterns were simple geometric designs, large and bold, free from tiny details. The Indians made their designs with red, yellow, blue, green, brown, and black paints.

Materials you will need:
A piece of flexible leather, suede, or tan-colored felt or stiff paper, approximately 18 by 14 inches (45 by 35 cm), acrylic or tempera paints, brushes, spray varnish or fixative, rawhide shoestring, awl or paper punch, scissors, paper, pencil, spray starch

1. To stiffen the felt, spray with starch and iron it.

2. To make a parfleche, follow the design shown in Figure 1.

Figure 1

3. Fold the piece crosswise as shown in Figure 2 to mark the center of the sides.

4. Draw curved sides as shown in Figure 2. Draw the outline on your piece of leather, felt, or paper.

5. Cut around the curved lines.

6. Turn the piece over and decorate it (Figure 3).

7. Fold the sides down (Figure 4).

8. Use an awl or paper punch to punch holes in the ends of the shape where indicated (Figure 4).

9. Tie the rawhide shoestring through the holes on each side, then fold in the ends until they meet, as in Figure 5.

10. Tie the rawhide to hold the parfleche closed, as shown in Figure 6.

1. To make a pouch, follow the diagram in Figure 7. Draw the outlines on your piece of leather or paper.

2. Cut out the design you have drawn. Turn the piece over and decorate it. Fold up the pouch.

3. Punch holes in the sides with an awl or paper punch, as in Figure 8.

4. Cut very narrow strips of leather (or use yarn, ribbons, or rawhide shoestring).

5. Tie in the fringe strips as shown in Figure 8.

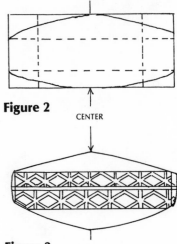

Figure 2 CENTER

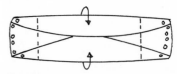

Figure 3

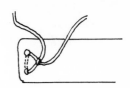

Figure 4

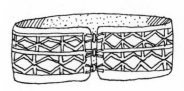

Figure 5

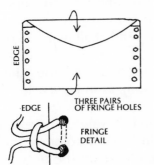

Figure 8

EDGE

EDGE · | THREE PAIRS OF FRINGE HOLES

FRINGE DETAIL

Figure 6

Figure 7

Toys and Games

Although life was not easy for North American Indians, children—and adults—participated in many games and played with toys. Usually the games helped develop skills that could be used later on: counting and throwing, for example. At the first Thanksgiving feast in 1621, the Indians there taught the settlers their games, and together they raced, wrestled, sang, and danced.

THE INDIAN NUT GAME

Materials you will need:
Four flat-sided nuts (such as almonds with shells on) or four clean, dried peach or apricot pits, tempera paint and brush or colored felt pens, shallow bowl or dish

1. Paint one side of each nut or pit red, the other blue (or any other color combination), as in Figure 1.

2. Give each color a number value. For example, red equals 2, blue equals 1. Instead of coloring the sides of the nuts, you can paint numbers on the nuts.

3. When the nuts are dry, place them in a bowl.

4. Each player takes a turn tossing nuts in a bowl one at a time. The colored side or number that falls face up gives the player's score. For example, if one red is up and three blues are up, the score is 5. The highest score for each round wins.

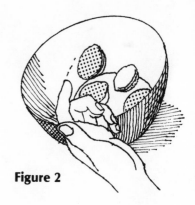

Figure 2

AMERICAN INDIAN STONE TOSS

Materials you will need:
Six flat rocks about as big as your hand, eighteen stones about the size of walnuts

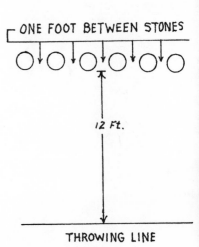

This game should only be played outdoors!
1. Arrange six flat rocks roughly 1 foot (0.3 m) apart in a row on the ground.

2. Put a smaller stone on top of each flat stone.

3. Give each player six small stones.

4. Each player, in turn, should stand behind a throwing line 12 feet (3.6 m) away and toss his or her six stones, trying to knock the small stone off the larger, flat stone. Observers must stand out of the line of fire!

Figure 1

5. Score 5 points for each stone knocked off. The highest score wins the game.

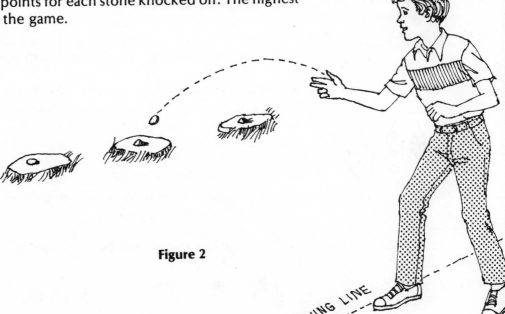

Figure 2

Indian War Bonnet

Indians wore many kinds of headdresses made from a wide variety of materials. Different tribes made head coverings from deerskin and antlers, animal heads, fur, wood, copper, and buffalo horns. The Sioux originated beautiful war bonnets out of headbands decorated with feathers. Each feather on a warrior's headdress represented a brave deed, or *coup*. Some bonnets even had long feather trains that hung down in back. The most elaborate headdresses were worn only on ceremonial occasions.

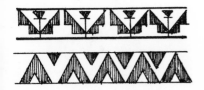

Figure 1

Materials you will need:
Construction paper, flexible cardboard or stiff fabric, tape measure, scissors, stapler, needle and thread, glue, feathers or feather shapes cut from construction paper

1. With a tape measure, measure around your head just above your ears. Add 2 inches (5 cm) for the overlap fastening. This will give you the total length of the piece.

2. Cut a strip of paper or fabric 1½ inches (3.75 cm) wide by (for example) 23 inches (57.5 cm) long. To fasten, wrap the strip around your head and overlap it for a snug fit. Remove the band and staple or sew the ends together.

3. Decorate the front of the band with Indian motifs (Figure 1).

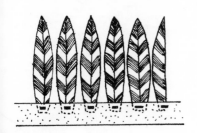

Figure 2

4. Use real feathers or cut about seventeen feather shapes.

5. Staple or glue the bases of the feathers side by side along the inside of the entire headband as in Figure 2.

6. Make a single feathered tail that hangs down the back by attaching feathers to a strip of paper or cloth about 10 inches (25 cm) long. Then attach the strip to the headband at the back.

Figure 3

7. Make side disks about 2 inches (5 cm) across, and decorate them with bits of feather that hang down. Attach the feather to the disk and then fasten the disk to the side of the headband (Figure 3).

Iroquois Tomahawk

A tomahawk is a short, hand-held axe that some Indian tribes used as a battle weapon. Braves carried their tomahawks in straps around their waists. The earliest tomahawks had blades made from stone, but after the Europeans introduced metal items, iron or steel blades were used.

Materials you will need:
A straight, heavy stick about 1½ inches (3.75 cm) around and 12 inches (30 cm) long (an old mop or broom handle would be good), a flat stone roughly triangular in shape, and about 9 to 10 inches (23 to 25 cm) long and 4 to 5 inches (10 to 13 cm) wide, heavy cardboard, rawhide shoestring or heavy cloth tape

1. For the tomahawk blade, use either a flat stone or a piece of heavy cardboard cut into a triangular shape.

2. Attach the rock or cardboard blade to the stick handle by wrapping cloth or rawhide around it about 3 inches (7.6 cm) from the sharpest point of the triangle, as in Figure 1.

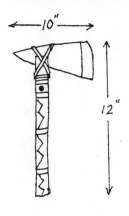

Figure 1

25

Indian Foods

The Indians used the leaves, roots, bark, flowers, fruits, and seeds of many wild plants for food. They knew which were safe and which were poisonous, and they knew how to extract poisons from some of the inedible ones to make them safe to eat. The Indians of Virginia shared their corn, squash, and beans with the first settlers in the 1600s. And the Indians of other North, Central, and South American lands gave us plants commonly used today around the world: pumpkins, tomatoes, peppers, peanuts, strawberries, Jerusalem artichokes, both white and sweet potatoes, cocoa, vanilla, and sunflowers.

The Indians ate or made drinks from wild herbs, barks, and roots that supplied many nutrients which saved the lives of many early settlers. Roots and herbs were chewed or powdered and boiled. Mixed with fats, they were made into healing salves. Various substances were used as chewing gums to relieve sores of the mouth or toothache, headache, and indigestion. Black birch bark was a favorite.

NORTHEAST INDIAN
CORN AND NUT PUDDING

Ingredients:
3 tablespoons yellow cornmeal (45 ml)
1 cup boiling water (250 ml)
2 tablespoons hickory nut or walnut butter (30 ml) (see nut butter recipe)
2 tablespoons maple syrup or honey (30 ml)
2 large eggs, beaten
1½ cups corn kernels, cooked (375 ml; 315 g)
½ cup hickory nuts or walnuts, shelled and chopped (125 ml; 105 g)

1. Mix cornmeal with boiling water in a bowl.

2. Stir in nut butter and maple syrup or honey, beating it until it cools slightly.

Figure 1

3. Beat in eggs, stirring them constantly so they do not harden.

4. Add corn and chopped nuts.

5. Pour the mixture into a buttered, 1-quart (1-l) casserole and sprinkle some chopped nuts on top.

6. Bake 35 to 45 minutes at 350°F (177°C).

7. Serve warm.

Figure 2

NUT BUTTER

Ingredients:
nuts*
maple syrup, honey, or cooking oil

1. Pound or chop ½ cup (125 ml; 105 g) of chopped nuts at a time into a paste. Half a cup of chopped nuts will make about ¼ cup (60 ml) of butter.

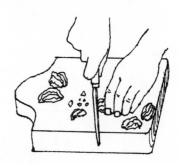

*Use dried, shelled peanuts, walnuts, black walnuts, hickory nuts, almonds, hazelnuts, or filberts.

Figure 1

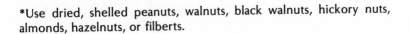

Figure 2

2. Add a few drops of oil, maple syrup, or honey as needed to make the mixture creamy.

3. Serve the nut butter on bread or toast, as a topping for cake or cookies, or mixed into recipes (see Corn and Nut Pudding).

TOASTED PUMPKIN OR SQUASH SEEDS

Ingredients:
pumpkin or squash seeds
oil
salt
mint or oregano

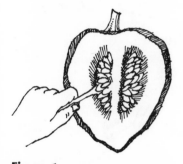

Figure 1

1. Remove seeds from the fruit and pull off the membranes.

2. Wash and dry the seeds.

3. Spread the clean seeds on a baking sheet or (if using a campfire) a flat rock.

4. Sprinkle about one tablespoon (15 ml) of cooking oil over the seeds. Set the baking sheet in the oven and bake at 325°F (163°C) for about 20 to 30 minutes until the seeds are dry and crisp.

Figure 2

5. Remove the seeds from the heat.

6. To add to the flavor, the Indians sprinkled the seeds with leaves of oregano or mint or coltsfoot. You can also sprinkle the seeds with salt.

7. Store the toasted seeds in an airtight container.

Index

Hopi Kachina Dolls

The Hopi Indians are one of the Pueblo groups of northern Arizona and New Mexico. The Hopi and other Pueblo tribes, including the Zuni, have ceremonies in which male dancers, called *kachinas*, wear masks and sing as they represent supernatural beings. Kachina dolls symbolize these religious figures. They are given to children not to play with, but to study. Traditionally, male members of the family—fathers and uncles—make the kachina dolls to give to the children. The dolls are hung up on the walls or rafters of the Hopi home, so they may be seen by the children at all times. The dolls teach children about the appearance of the different kachinas as part of their religious training.

The dried roots of dead cottonwood trees—found along the banks of the Little Colorado River—are the basic material for the dolls. The wood is sawed, whittled with a penknife, modeled with a chisel and wood rasp, and then smoothed and sanded with a piece of sandstone. Details of the head and face are whittled from wood and fastened with tiny pegs or glue. Traditional kachina doll makers cover the doll with a flat white layer of kaolin, a clay substance. Colored paints are added over the white base surface. Paints are made from minerals and earth pigments, soot or corn smut. Green, blue, black, red, yellow, and white are the main colors used.

Kachina masks are not realistic, but represent the *spirit* of the object. Visual clues are given by signs (a bear paw track, an ear of corn) as well as by the colors used. The color used on a kachina mask is symbolic. Colors tell the direction from which the kachina came. The Hopi have six directional colors: yellow means north or northwest, blue-green means west or southwest, red means south or southeast, and white means east or northeast. Black stands for down, and all the colors together refer to the zenith, or up.

The Hopi believe that the costumed kachinas carry the prayers of the people to the gods. Hopi have over two hundred kachinas and invent new ones all the time. Some kachinas represent good spirits, others demons or ogres.

The mask, colors, the motifs on the sides and top of the head, the shape and color of different body parts and other markings identify the kachinas.

In addition to the three-dimensional carved dolls, infants are given simplified versions of kachinas made from a single piece of flat board. The flat kachina doll shows only the most essential details of the particular kachina, a kind of "shorthand" doll. Our models will be one flat doll and one fully modeled one. Authentic kachinas vary in size from 3 to 4 inches (7.6 to 10 cm) tall to 8 to 9 inches (20 to 23 cm).

Materials you will need:
a cylinder of balsa wood, self-hardening clay, modeling tools or a whittling knife, tempera paints, brushes, cloth scraps, feathers, glue

A. Full-size Kachina doll
1. Follow Figure 1 to form the basic body shapes out of clay or wood to make an 8-inch (20-cm) figure.

2. Glue the spool-shaped head to the body cylinder.

3. Glue on the legs. If you want, the legs can be simply painted on the bottom section of the body cylinder instead of separately carved or modeled.

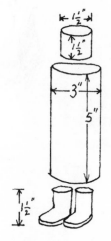

Figure 1

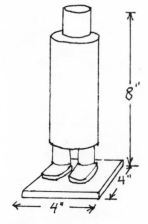

Figure 2

4. Glue pieces to a stand roughly 4 inches (10 cm) squa for stability, as in Figure 2. Let the glue dry.

5. Paint features on the doll, using designs from the s bols and sketches shown below.

6. Glue bits of cloth on the figure to represent loin or cape, skirts, etc., as in Figure 3.

7. Glue feathers on the head or make tiny holes head to hold the feathers, as in Figure 4.

Commonly Used Mask Symbols

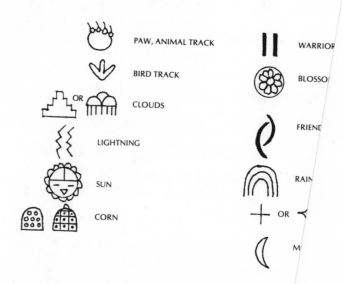

PAW, ANIMAL TRACK   WARRIOR

BIRD TRACK   BLOSSO

CLOUDS

LIGHTNING   FRIEN

SUN   RAIN

CORN

B. Infants' Kachina doll
1. Model a wooden or clay slab about (12.7 by 8 cm) and roughly ¼ to ½ inch thick, as in Figure 5.

2. Paint designs on the slab, as in Figur on top of the head, fastening them on